KU-787-555

PAINTBALL

FOR FUN!

By Pamela Dell

Content Adviser: William Roper, Ph.D., Founder of Paintball Program and First Coach,
Wasatch Academy, Mt. Pleasant, Utah
Reading Adviser: Susan Kesselring, M.A., Literacy Educator, Rosemount-Apple Valley-Eagan (Minnesota) School District

Compass Point Books ✦ Minneapolis, Minnesota

Compass Point Books
151 Good Counsel Drive
P.O. Box 669
Mankato, MN 56002-0669

Copyright © 2009 by Compass Point Books
All rights reserved. No part of this book may be reproduced without written permission from the publisher. The publisher takes no
responsibility for the use of any of the materials or methods described in this book, nor for the products thereof.
Printed in the United States of America.

This book was manufactured with paper containing
at least 10 percent post-consumer waste.

Photographs ©: Mary Gascho/iStockphoto, cover (left); Eileen Meyer/Shutterstock, cover (right), back cover; Maksim Shmeljov/Fotolia, 4–5; Ariel Bravy/Shutterstock,
5 (top); Tim Anderson/Rex USA, 6; Rex USA, 7; William Valentine/iStockphoto, 8, 47; vertigo77/Fotolia, 9, 33; Jason Maehl/Shutterstock, 10; Abel Feyman/Shutterstock,
11 (top); Alexander Kalina/Shutterstock, 11 (bottom), 12; 2008 Jupiterimages Corporation, 13, 44; Jozsef Szasz-Fabian/iStockphoto, 14; Flashon Studio/Shutterstock,
15 (top); Maksim Shmeljov/BigStockPhoto, 15 (bottom); Ron Buskirk/Alamy, 16; Dariush M./Shutterstock, 18–19 (all), 20 (bottom), 31; jeanma85/Fotolia, 20–21;
Sean Murphy/Riser/Getty Images, 22–23; Max Tactic/Fotolia, 23 (right), 30, 34; Chris McGrath/Getty Images, 24–25 (all); Igor Terekhov/123RF, 26; Masturawati Asari/
Shutterstock, 27; Paulo Oliveira/Shutterstock, 28 (bottom), 36–37; Darcy Finley/Fotolia, 28–29; Scott Peterson/Getty Images, 35; Spencer Platt/Getty Images, 36 (bottom);
Bea Youngs, 38, 41 (right); Derek Yegan/Shutterstock, 39; AP Images/Chris Park, 40, 43 (top); Thomas Concordia/WireImage/Getty Images, 41 (left); Tom Shaw/Getty
Images, 42 (top); Arkansas Democrat-Gazette, 42 (bottom); David Crausby/Alamy, 43 (bottom); dotshock/Fotolia, 45.

Editor: Brenda Haugen
Page Production: The Design Lab
Photo Researcher: Eric Gohl
Art Director: LuAnn Ascheman-Adams
Creative Director: Keith Griffin
Editorial Director: Nick Healy
Managing Editor: Catherine Neitge

Library of Congress Cataloging-in-Publication Data
Dell, Pamela.
  Paintball for fun! / by Pamela Dell.
      p. cm. — (For fun)
  Includes index.
  ISBN 978-0-7565-3863-7 (library binding)
1. Paintball (Game)—Juvenile literature. I. Title. II. Series.
  GV1202.S87D46 2009
  796.2—dc22   2008007718

Visit Compass Point Books on the Internet at www.compasspointbooks.com
or e-mail your request to custserv@compasspointbooks.com

Table of Contents

Note: In this book, there are two kinds of vocabulary words. Paintball Words to Know are words specific to paintball. They are defined on page 46. Other Words to Know are helpful words that are not related only to paintball. They are defined on page 47.

An Exciting New Sport

Game on! At the sound of the referee's shrill whistle, you and the other players scatter into the woods. You're wearing boots, gloves, goggles, a face mask, and long sleeves. Your clothes are the colors of the woods, making it easier to hide. And you do want to stay hidden. It's a matter of survival.

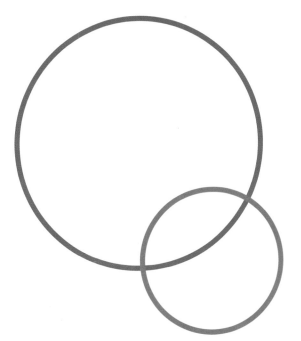

The minute someone spots you, you're in danger. An enemy might take you out with a single, well-aimed blast of his or her "marker." But don't sweat it too much. That blast will come in the form of a bright-colored splotch of paint. Getting marked by paint is a big deal in one important way, though. It signals you're out of the game. This is the thrill and challenge of paintball. You want to get others with your paintball marker before they get you. Those who play love the rush—the pure excitement—of paintball's fast-moving action. No wonder it's one of the fastest-growing sports in the world!

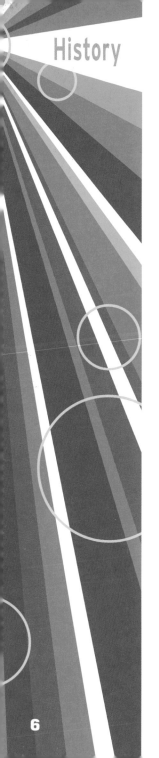

From Experiment to Explosion

The first paintball game was played in 1981 in the New Hampshire woods. Since then, paintball's popularity has exploded around the world.

The sport began with three friends who were interested in "survival" games. Hayes Noel, Charles Gaines, and Bob Gurnsey came up with the idea of stalking one another through the woods using markers that shot balls of paint. Their game, which they called Survival, was basically a tag game. Once a player was hit with a splotch of paint, he was out.

On June 27, 1981, the three friends gathered with nine other men to play Survival in the New Hampshire woods. Armed with paintball markers, compasses, maps, and a dozen flags, the men played a type of capture-the-flag game. The last one standing after three hours was Ritchie White. He captured most of the flags and never got hit—and he hadn't even fired a single shot!

The next year, Gurnsey opened the first commercial paintball field. He called paintball the National Survival Game (NSG). Slowly, interest in the sport grew. Soon it was known simply as paintball. From the United States, the paintball craze spread to Canada and throughout the world.

Today paintball is a big business. More than 40 million people in about 200 countries now play the game.

A New Use

Paintball markers didn't start out as game equipment. The markers used in the New Hampshire woods to play Survival were designed to mark stray cattle or trees that needed to be cut down.

What It's All About

Think of paintball as tag, cops-and-robbers, and hide-and-seek all rolled into one—but more advanced. You try to stay hidden from your opponents while doing your best to sneak up and blast them.

In the sport's early days, most people played games like the one in New Hampshire. Each player was out to win for himself or herself. Now the most popular paintball games are played by teams. Most of these team games are based on a capture-the-flag model. Each team tries to steal flags and hang them at its own base. But no matter what style of game you like, there's one basic rule that always applies: One paintball splotch and you're out!

The best and safest place to play paintball is at a facility designed for the sport. Commercial paintball fields rent equipment and offer food, water, and bathrooms. They also provide referees to keep every game safe and fair. These facilities usually have several types of fields, allowing for lots of game options. Whether you play with friends or team up with strangers, playing on these specially designed fields is a blast!

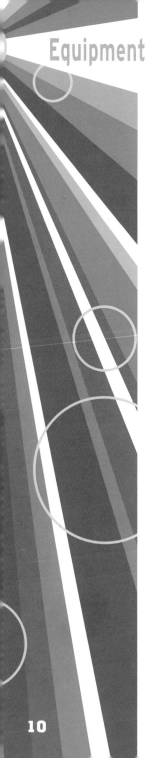

Gearing Up

You can't play without equipment. Two of the main pieces of equipment are paintballs and a paintball marker, which fires the paintballs. If you're just starting out, your best bet is to rent your marker and other gear at the field where you play. That way you'll get a feel for the different options out there. And there are a lot of them.

You don't need anything fancy to have fun playing paintball. If you'd rather buy than rent, some stores and online sites offer fairly inexpensive gear for beginners.

Paintball pellets come in many bright colors and look like bath oil beads. They're made of thin gelatin skins filled with liquid that's nontoxic and Earth-friendly. When the paintball hits a target it splits open, leaving a splash of color. If you wash yourself and your clothes soon after you're done playing, the paint rinses off easily. However, if you let the paint stay on your clothes too long, it will stain them.

You'll also need a hopper. The hopper attaches to the marker and holds your paintballs. Each time you fire your marker, another paintball drops down from the hopper into the marker so you are ready to fire again.

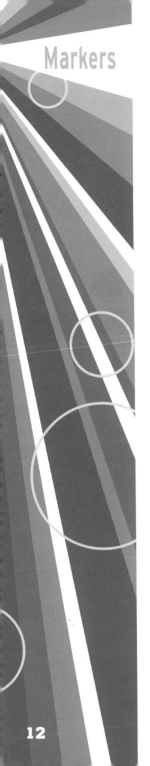

Your Best Shot

Paintball markers come in many styles, designs, and prices. Some look like small handguns. Others look more like big, high-powered rifles. But the idea is still the same. Each time a marker is fired, a blast of either compressed air or a gas called nitrogen pushes a paintball down the barrel and out into the air like a bullet.

The air or nitrogen is contained in a tank that's usually directly attached to the marker. Some expert players, however, carry their air supplies on their backs in packs or harnesses with tubes that send the air into their markers.

The two most commonly used paintball markers are the pump marker and the semiautomatic. Pump markers are usually the least expensive. They are accurate and easy to use. This makes them the best choice for beginners. With pump markers, each paintball is "pumped" into the barrel by hand, one at a time.

Semiautomatics are popular with experienced paintballers. They have sensitive triggers so no pumping action is required. They fire fast and often. Instead of loading manually, the paintballs drop down for firing as fast as you can pull the trigger.

Electronic paintball markers are the wave of the future. These markers have built-in computer chips that control firing. Many are fully automatic. That means they will keep blasting paintballs as long as the trigger is held down. This may add thrills to the game, but an automatic marker gives a player a big advantage because it fires much faster than other markers. Automatic markers are rarely allowed in organized games or tournaments.

Obey the Law

Always check the laws in your area. In most places it's illegal to carry a piece of equipment that looks like a bullet-firing gun, even if it isn't one. So if it's not in a carrying case, don't tote your paintball marker in public—not even on a playground or in a park.

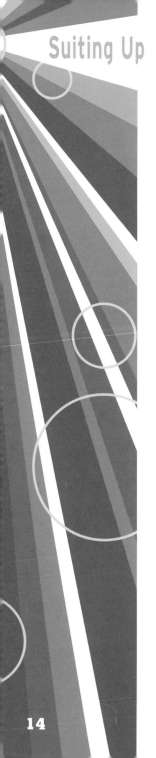

What to Wear

Paintball is one of the safest sports around, but you have to dress for the game. Eye and head protection are vital.

Face mask and goggles: You must wear a face mask and good-fitting goggles that are approved for paintball play. Only goggles specially made for the sport can stand up to the speed of flying paintballs. Getting hit in the eye with a paintball can cause severe injury or even blindness. Wearing a face mask protects your ears and the rest of your face. A player won't be allowed on a commercial playing field without these two important pieces of equipment.

Shoes: Wear shoes that provide good ankle support. You'll avoid sprains and strains that could result from a lot of running and ducking on uneven terrain. Most players wear hiking boots, sports shoes with cleats, or high-top tennis shoes. The more experience you have on different types of turf (dirt, rocky hillsides, or fake grass, for instance), the easier it will be to decide what type of shoes will help your game the most.

Clothes: The clothes you wear are up to you—and the weather. Generally, loose-fitting clothes are most comfortable and better for quick movements. Long sleeves and long pants are recommended. You probably don't want to wear bright, easy-to-spot colors since being sneaky is a big advantage. When playing in the woods, most paintballers choose earth tones or camouflage gear. Gloves are another smart choice. Paintballs rarely break the skin, but they can sting when they hit and sometimes cause bruising.

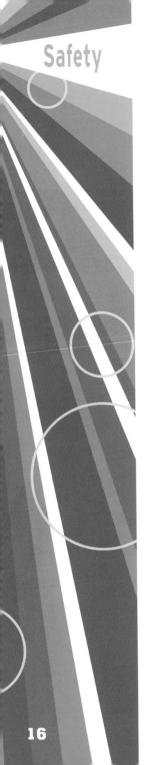

Important Tips

Paintball is a safe sport if you keep a few pointers in mind:

- Handle your marker with care at all times. Never fire it in places where people aren't wearing paintball safety gear.

- Whenever you're off the playing field, you must use a barrel blocking device (BBD) or the more modern barrel sock to plug the barrel of your marker. The BBD keeps paintballs from escaping if the marker is accidentally fired.

- Always keep your trigger in the locked or "safe" position when you are not playing. Even if the air tank is removed, some markers can still shoot paintballs unexpectedly and hurt someone.

- Don't set your marker to fire at speeds above the set limit, which is usually no more than 300 feet (91.4 meters) per second. Although markers can be adjusted to fire faster, this is a major rule violation at commercial paintball facilities, and your marker will be checked. So don't even think about it!

- Goggles aren't just for the playing field. Always wear them when you're loading, cleaning, or doing other work on your marker. And even if you are wearing goggles, never look down an uncovered marker barrel.

- Stay alert for dangers on the field, such as sharp rocks, broken glass, or other possible hazards.

A Safe Game

Some people object to paintball because they believe it's dangerous or warlike. Some fear the war-games nature of the sport increases players' aggressive behavior. In reality, neither of these things is true. The paintball industry has safety standards that are strictly followed. According to a study by the National Injury Information Clearinghouse of the U.S. Consumer Product Safety Commission, fewer injuries are reported in paintball than in sports such as basketball, baseball, and even bowling.

On the Field

Who's out there on the field during a paintball game? At some levels, such as collegiate or professional, paintball teams often include team captains and coaches. But the most important part of the support system during a game is the referees.

A player gets some help from a coach.

The number of players in any paintball game may vary, but each team starts out with the same count. Some types of games have as few as five players per team; others may have hundreds.

In capture-the-flag games, whoever grabs a flag is called the flag runner. In these games, there are usually both defensive and offensive players. Defensive players stay close to their team's flags to defend them from their opponents. Offensive players work to steal the enemy's flags, so they usually see a little bit more action.

A paintball referee

Referees are paintball's bosses. They keep the game safe and fun, check faulty equipment, and make sure everybody's playing fairly. On a big playing field, referees can't always see everything that happens. But if a ref calls you out, don't argue. Just leave the field and wait until your next game.

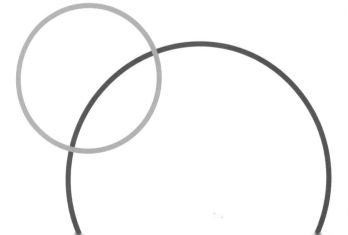

Play Smart and Play Fair

If you're at least 10 years old, you can play at a paintball facility. But are you cunning enough? Paintball involves being sly and sneaky. It also helps if you can make quick decisions.

Paintball is usually played in teams. To win, you and your teammates need to work together—outsmarting your opponents and backing each other up.

Paintball isn't a contact sport. Players must stay away from members of the opposing team—at least 5 feet (1.5 m) away on most fields. If you accidentally get closer, move away at once or you both risk being eliminated. And never fire at a referee!

Each paintball game usually lasts between 15 and 30 minutes. Most teams play several games. But in any game, you're out as soon as you're hit by a paintball splatter. If the paintball hits you but doesn't break, you've lucked out. If it does break, either on your body or equipment, you must raise your marker, yell "Hit," "Out," or "Dead man," and get off the field.

Playing fairly is important. Players who wipe off the paint so they can keep playing or cheat in other ways are not respected. "Wiping" will get a player thrown out of a game. If it happens more than once, a player may be banned forever from a commercial paintball field. Being honest is what it's all about in this sport.

Paint Check

If you call yourself out and then discover you haven't really been hit, too bad! You're still out. So be sure you've been hit before speaking up. If you aren't sure, call in a referee for a "splat" check.

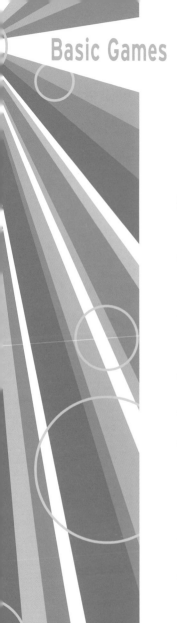

Capture the Flag

The first multiplayer paintball game was a form of capture the flag. But it was still every man for himself. Paintball is more of a team sport now, but capture the flag is still an exciting way to play. There are lots of variations. The basic idea is that each team tries to steal the opponents' flags and hang them at its own base, or flag station. Players move around the field as they work to claim flags. They take cover behind large natural barriers or man-made objects called bunkers. After getting a flag, a player still has to get back to base without being tagged.

Sometimes each team has one flag. In other games, each team has many flags. In yet another type of game, many flags are staked around the field, and the team that manages to capture the most wins the game. A team gets points for each flag it steals and for every opponent it eliminates from play. To win, a team must capture all the flags or tag all the members of the opposing team.

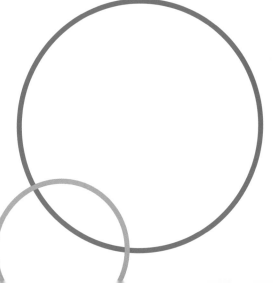

What's the Story?

Do you want to play paintball games that have stories behind them? Then scenario games may be for you. A scenario game usually has a basic storyline—a plot that has already been worked out. Players may act out real-life war battles or other events from history.

Other scenario games have fictional themes—action that's entirely made up. Such games may center on a fantasy world, a futuristic outer space environment, or even a spooky zombie story. Whether based on fiction or nonfiction, scenario games often go on for hours. Sometimes games last into the night or are scheduled entirely after dark. If a player gets tagged, he or she is out of the game for a set period of time before he or she can start playing again.

Scenario players usually wear costumes and portray characters. The playing area may have many props, such as hidden treasures or secret documents that give the finder an advantage.

Some classic scenario games include spy versus spy, protect the president, and rescue a pilot downed in enemy territory. Scenario games are only limited by the imagination of those who think them up.

Turn Up the Intensity!

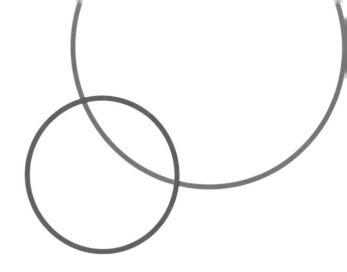

Speedball is mostly a tournament game. It's often the main type of paintball offered at indoor facilities. Speedball is a high-powered, high-speed capture-the-flag game. It's played on a smaller field with bunkers of all kinds. Teams start within shooting distance of each other and move up the field toward a single flag. Each

team's goal is to hang that flag at its own base before the other team does.

Strategy, timing, and teamwork are vital in speedball—as is seeking cover behind the bunkers. In this game, you never want to be out in the open for very long. Speedball relies a lot on snap shooting—briefly popping out from behind a bunker to tag an opponent before hiding behind the bunker again. Good aim is important. Speedball is the game of the paintball pros, but amateurs love its fast-paced, thrilling action, too.

The Speedball Field

A typical speedball field is no larger than half a football field. Most of the bunkers are inflatable objects of all sizes and shapes. The bunker types include the cone, the temple, the snake, and the Dorito, which is shaped like the triangular chips called Doritos.

Think Quick!

Xball paintball is another form of capture the flag. It is played in several short, fast segments. Two teams compete against each other. Each team includes five people. As a time clock ticks off the minutes, the two teams try to capture a flag stationed in the middle of the field.

Each game segment lasts until one team steals the flag and hangs it at its base. The team capturing the flag earns one point.

After a team captures the flag, everybody takes a three-minute break. Then a new game segment begins. The same players might compete again, or a team might substitute new players for each segment. After a total of 22 minutes, time's up, and the entire game is done.

Paintball on Television

In the fall of 2007, the Fox Sports Network aired a 13-episode series called *Xtreme Paintball: Beyond the Paint*. It featured nine of the sport's hottest American pro players. Between the Xball segments, the series showed interviews and close-up looks into the lives of these exciting players.

Tactical Dos and Don'ts

Paintball is a game of stealth. That means being sneaky and staying quiet most of the time. Don't show that you're a "squid," or beginner, by hooting and hollering across the field like some new players do.

Other signs of a squid are firing like crazy the moment the game begins or shooting off paintballs without a target in sight. This only wastes your paint.

You don't want to get so excited that you hit your own team members. However, even experienced players sometimes hit their own teammates by mistake. It's often hard to identify who's in front of you before you

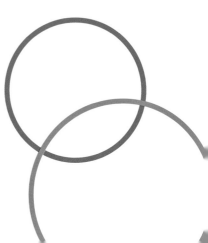

pull the trigger. To make it easier, teams sometimes wear armbands of the same color. They also might have a code word or phrase that they say to prove they're playing for the same team.

Different types of games require different moves. Focus more on hitting opponents than staying safe yourself. Don't just take cover behind a bunker and hope to get a few good shots. Think like a hunter. Go after your "prey" instead of just waiting for them to appear. But always stay alert to what's happening around you.

Some players prefer sneaky moves. They lurk, crawl, or slip quickly from one safe spot to the next. Others take a more explosive approach—like making a crazy run right out in the open. Rushing like this draws attention, which can be risky. But it also can

give your teammates a chance to fire on players who aren't watching them. You'll find your style once you've played a few times.

Time's Up!

If only a few minutes remain in the game, don't be shy! Make a mad dash for the flag. Take a risk. Try to get some hits. What have you got to lose with so little time left?

Keeping Your Gear in Great Shape

Getting involved in paintball can be costly. There are many things to consider when you decide to buy your own gear. You also need to take care of that gear to keep it working properly and keep everyone safe.

- Beginners should buy an inexpensive marker. Most manufacturers provide care and cleaning instructions along with the equipment. Learning to clean and care for a less-expensive marker is better than worrying about damaging one that cost a lot of money. When you're more experienced, you can consider buying a better marker.

- Clean your marker regularly to keep it firing smoothly. If something happens to your equipment on the field, alert the referee right away.

- Never leave your marker in the sun or where it's hot—like in the trunk of a car in the summer. In high temperatures, the gas in your air tank can expand and even explode.

- Don't let your paintballs bask in the sun either. Heat can cause them to lose their shape, get sticky, and create quite a mess.

- Carefully inspect your goggles for cracks or other damage before you play. If your goggles attach to a face mask, make sure you can't push them out of the mask.

- Before you play, treat your goggles with a "no-fog" product so you won't have to leave the game because you can't see.

- Always wipe down the insides of your mask and goggles after you play.

Better Safe Than Sorry

If your marker or your air tank gets damaged, the safest thing to do is to take it to an airsmith, a person trained to work on paintball markers. Trying to repair your own equipment can be dangerous.

Outdoor and Indoor Fun

Paintball fields operate all over the United States and Canada. Both indoor and outdoor facilities offer lots of game-playing options.

Paintball played in a natural landscape, like that first game in New Hampshire, is known today as woodsball. The turf might be all woodlands, or it might include fields, swamps, and even mountains or canyons.

Some outdoor paintball fields have settings that look more civilized. Some look like deserted towns or military bases.

Paintball fields that use man-made barriers are often called Sup-Air fields because of the inflatable bunkers. These fields are usually designed for games such as speedball, and they can be found at both outdoor and indoor facilities.

Playing indoors can provide a lot of different experiences. Indoor paintball facilities are as different as the buildings that house them. Some facilities are giant warehouses with lots of

space to roam. Others are buildings with many floors. Opponents can chase their enemies from level to level. Some paintball facilities have underground areas with lots of tunnels and winding hallways. Usually you're in for a lot of suspense and surprises.

Options for Die-hard Fans

The sport of paintball has really grown. There's a wide world of fun beyond the local paintball field. Paintball fanatics can get more of their passion on television, the Internet, and in video games. There are many magazines, podcasts, blogs, DVDs, YouTube videos, and even a video-on-demand TV channel devoted to paintball. You also can check in with many professional paintball teams on their MySpace pages.

of friends to play as often as possible at your local facility. Learn how to play safe and work well together. Sharpen your skills and tactics. Employees at your paintball field can probably tell you if there are any nearby paintball leagues or regional competitions for people your age. Organized leagues and tournaments guarantee that you'll be playing against people at your own skill level.

Maybe you're wondering if you could ever make it as a pro paintballer. Keep in mind that every member of a professional team began by playing for fun—just like you are!

Live-action tournaments are held all over the world. They are geared to every level. If you'd like to play in a tournament someday, look around you. Start by organizing a group

Paintball's Big Leagues

Paintball leagues are forming all over the world. In the United States, there are regional amateur leagues, college leagues, semipro leagues, and a few professional paintball leagues. Of these pro leagues, the National Professional Paintball League (NPPL) is the oldest and best known.

The NPPL was started in 1992 by a group of experienced paintball players, both amateur and professional. One of the

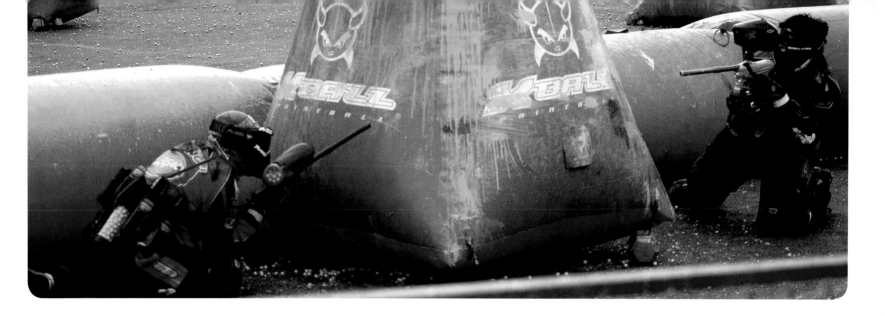

NPPL's main purposes was to make the public more aware of paintball. The group staged tournaments with strict rules, cash prizes, and fair, qualified referees.

The NPPL has gone through some ups and downs since it began, but now it's well established. The five annual tournaments the group sponsors are very popular. Professional, semiprofessional, and amateur teams come from all over to compete with teams at similar skill levels. The winning pro team might go home with as much as $100,000 or more.

The National Xball League (NXL) formed in 2003. It has increased interest in paintball even more. The NXL was created to get television airtime for the Xball format of the game. TV paintball broadcasts are a dream come true for paintball fanatics across the country. And they continue to be an eye-opener for those who tune in not realizing how fun paintball can be.

Famous Faces in Paintball

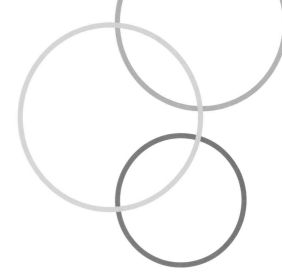

They've got names like Rock-It Kids and Naughty Dogs. Though some of the team names may be funny, those who play paintball professionally take the sport seriously. The hottest pro teams and players are turning paintball into a sport that growing numbers of people are enjoying.

Team Dynasty

In 2001, San Diego's Team Dynasty made a big bang in its first season. It won the NPPL World Cup that year—something a first-year team had never done. Dynasty has continued to

awe fans ever since, breaking records and achieving many major wins.

Alex Lundqvist

Alex Lundqvist not only looks like a supermodel, he is one! Born April 14, 1972, in Sweden, he started modeling at the suggestion of his girlfriend. But his modeling career hasn't stopped his passion for extreme sports. Lundqvist has tried snowboarding and skydiving but thinks there's nothing more exciting than paintball. Today he makes his home in New York and plays paintball with the NPPL's Jersey Authority as well as for an NXL team called the Russian Legion.

Bea Youngs

Bea Youngs is among the best-known female paintballers. She got her start in 2000 when she became part of the newly forming team the Femmes Fatales. Today she's a member of Southern California's Team Destiny, which she also owns. Besides playing paintball and owning a team, Youngs is editor in chief for *Paintball Sports Magazine*. She also volunteers as a commentator at paintball sports events and teaches children at paintball camps. Youngs is married to her coach, pro paintballer Mike Paxson, who plays for the Los Angeles Ironmen.

What Happened When?

1970 — **1980** — **1981** — **1982** — **1983** — **1984** — **1985**

1974 James Hale, an employee of the Daisy Manufacturing Company, designs and patents the first paintball marker for use in marking cattle and trees.

1982 Bob Gurnsey opens the first commercial outdoor paintball field, calling the game the National Survival Game, or NSG.

1985 Robert G. Shepherd designs the Splatmaster, the first marker created just for playing paintball.

1984 The first indoor paintball facility opens in Rochester, New York.

1983 The first NSG National Championships are held, with a $14,000 cash prize for the winner.

1981 The first game of paintball is played June 27 in the woods near Henniker, New Hampshire.

| 1988 | 1991 | 1992 | 1993 | 2000 | 2005 | 2010 |

1988 The International Paintball Players Association (IPPA) is founded to educate the public about the sport and promote its growth.

1992 The National Professional Paintball League (NPPL) is formed, replacing the IPPA.

2007 The NXL gets its own MySpace page, and the Fox Sports Network airs the 13-episode program *Xtreme Paintball: Beyond the Paint*.

2002 The National Xball League (NXL) forms to showcase the game of Xball on TV.

1993 Paintball comes to television, and interest in the sport takes a huge leap after the NPPL "DC Cup" tournament airs live on ESPN.

43

Fun Paintball Facts

Since 2000, the number of frequent paintball players—those playing 15 days a year or more—has more than doubled, going from 800,000 in 2000 to 2 million in 2005.

Paintballers spent $330 million on gear in 2005, more than was spent for any other sport except baseball and basketball.

In the late 1970s, before their famous 12-man paintball game in the woods, Charles Gaines and Hayes Noel tested paintball markers on themselves in a two-man game. With towels wrapped around their waists to soften the blows, they discovered that the paintball sting was bearable.

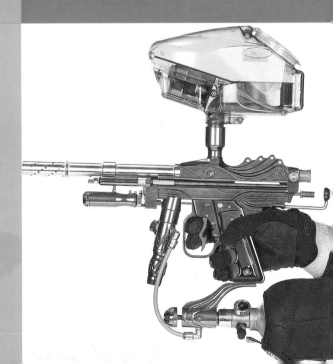

New Jersey was the last state to make paintball legal. The sport was outlawed there until 1988. Before then, anyone firing a paintball marker in the state could be arrested for assault and battery.

The Daisy Manufacturing Corporation—the first company to make paintball markers specially designed for paintballers—had another popular invention. The BB gun, an air-powered rifle, was made by the company beginning in the 1880s.

A women's paintball team called the Puffs was known to fire pink paintballs. The Puffs also added Chanel No. 5 perfume to their pink paintballs.

Team Dynasty earned the best three-year record of any team in paintball tournament history. Team Dynasty won four out of the five annual NPPL events in 2003, two NPPL events in 2004, and, in 2005, eight out of 10 national tournament events.

Paintball Words to Know

barrel: tube of a marker through which paintballs are released when the marker is fired

barrel blocking device (BBD): plug made of metal or plastic that fits into a marker barrel to prevent paintballs from being fired

barrel sock: nylon or cloth sleeve that fits around the end of a marker barrel to prevent paintballs from being fired

bunker: any object used as a barrier between paintball players

flag station: location of a team's base camp and flag during a capture-the-flag game

hit: when a paintball breaks anywhere on a player's body

marker: piece of equipment used to fire paintballs

snap shooting: jumping out from behind a bunker, taking a few fast shots, and then returning to the safety of the bunker

squid: new or inexperienced paintball player

wiping: cleaning a paint hit in order to stay in the game; considered cheating

Other Words to Know

amateur: playing a sport for fun rather than as a paying job

banned: not allowed

camouflage: blend in with the surroundings

canister: container

collegiate: having to do with college-level activities

fanatics: extremely enthusiastic, over-the-top fans

multiplayer: involving more than one player

nontoxic: not poisonous

stalking: going after someone in a sneaky manner

strategy: clever plan

terrain: ground or land

Where to Learn More

MORE BOOKS TO READ

Marx, Mandy R. *Paintball*. Mankato, Minn.: Capstone Press, 2006.

Roza, Greg. *Paintball: Rules, Tips, Strategy, and Safety*. New York: Rosen, 2007.

ON THE ROAD

Giant Paintball Park
88 Fair Drive
Costa Mesa, CA 92626
877/442-6897

Orbital Paintball Park
12771 N. Highway 301
Thonotosassa, FL 33592
813/789-8159

ON THE WEB

For more information on this topic, use FactHound.

1. Go to *www.facthound.com*
2. Type in this book ID: 0756538637
3. Click on the *Fetch It* button.

FactHound will find the best Web sites for you.

INDEX

ABOUT THE AUTHOR

Pamela Dell began her professional career writing for adults and started writing for children about 12 years ago. Since then she has published fiction and nonfiction books, written numerous magazine articles, and created award-winning interactive multimedia.